The Souls Journey after Death

An Abridgement of
Ibn Al-Qayyim's Kitabar-Ruh

With Commentary by
Layla Mabrouk

First Published © Dar Al Taqwa Ltd. 1987

Reprinted in 2011

ISBN 978-2-1-870582-05-6

All rights reserved. No Part of this publication may be reproduced, stored in a retrieval system or transmitted, in any form or by any means, electronic, mechanical, photocopying, recording or otherwise without the prior permission of the publishers.

Translation: Aisha Bewley

Editorial: Abdalhaqq Bewley

Published by:
Dar Al Taqwa Ltd.
7A, Melcombe Street
Baker Street
London
NW1 6AE

www.daraltagwa.com
e-mail: sales@daraltaqwa.com

Printed by:
IMAK OFFSET Printing Center
T: 0090 212 656 49 97
F: 0090 212 656 29 26
www.imakofset.com.tr
isa@imakofset.com.tr

بسم الله الرحمن الرحيم

" In the name of Allah the most merciful the compassionate"

'Every soul will taste death.'

(Qur'an 2:185)

CONTENTS

Introduction 1

From One World to Another! 5

The Meaning and Truth of Death 11

The Bliss of the Interspace between the
Two Worlds 15

The Punishment of the Interspace 21

How can a Man save Himself from the
Punishment of the Grave before it is
too late? 27

What can the Living do to Rescue the
Dead Person from Punishment? 31

Glossary 39

INTRODUCTION

'They will ask you about the spirit. Say, "The spirit is at the behest of your Lord. You have been given only a little knowledge."'[1]

'The living go on and the dead do not.' ... Allah! What an extraordinary expression and what an even stranger position to take. When somebody dies, our sorrow and tears, our weeping and mourning soon cease. The funeral rites, the Thursday ceremony and finally the forty-day ceremony are held and then all is forgotten. We say to ourselves, 'The living go on and the dead do not,' and put the dead person out of mind on the premise that he is dead and at rest. We forget or pretend to forget that he is in fact in even greater need of us than the living. He faces the future all alone, hidden away in the domain of the earthworms, buried under the earth in a desolate grave. He was in the light and now he is in darkness. He was surrounded by beauty and spaciousness and now he is enclosed in narrowness and gloom. He was in bliss and he now is in torment.

All this, however, is measured by criteria which are completely different from those that we, the living, use. We cannot perceive these things with our eyes or our inner senses or even our ears. The dead person is completely aware of them, but according to the criteria of the Next World. What are those criteria? What is death? What is life in the Next World...the world after death? Questions, many questions come to mind.

---

[1] Al-Isra (17): 85

I have read more than one book on this subject, but I consider my basic source in what I say here to be the *Kitab ar-Ruh* by Ibn al- Qayyim which is based on the Qur'an, the *Sunna*, Traditions and what the greatest scholars have said. However, before reading Ibn al- Qayyim, we must first know who Ibn al-Qayyim was, and whether he is a reliable source.

I will here present some of what I have read about Ibn al-Qayyim al-Jawziyya in a magisterial thesis submitted to Azhar University by Dr. Husayni 'Ali Ridwan. In it he points out that Ibn al-Qayyim's real name was Muhammad b. Abi Bakr b. Sa'id b. Hariz az-Zar'i, and then ad-Dimashqi. His title was Shamsu'd-din, and his *kunya* was Abu 'Abdullah. How then did he come by the name Ibn al-Qayyim al-Jawziyya? His father was the director of a school called al-Jawziyya which was located in the Damascus Wheat Market and for that reason he was called "Ibn al-Qayyim al-Jawziyya" or "Ibn al-Qayyim". He is not the same as Ibn al- Qayyim al-Jawzi who died in Baghdad in 597 A.H.

Ibn al-Qayyim al-Jawziyya was born into a scholarly and virtuous family in 691 A.H./1292 A.D. At that time Damascus was a centre of literature and thought. Many schools were located there and he studied and graduated under the protection, direction and sponsorship of his father. He was particularly influenced by his Shaykh and teacher Ahmad b. Taymiyyah, and also by Ibn ash-Shirazi amongst others.

When he had reached maturity and had become a scholar of weight and reputation, he started to teach at al-Jawziyya and had many students, including Ibn Kathir. He was looked to as a model in both youth and middle-age, by reason of the fact that he went out of his way to pass on to others the knowledge he had been given by those who came before him.

From his youth onwards he was constantly striving, tireless in his examination of everything around him, brilliant. Throughout his life, he remained an example of humility. He was calm and convivial, constant in worship, getting right to the core of the *deen*, a living example of the meaning of scrupulousness. He was courageous about stating the truth, no matter what the consequences.

I have put together all these qualities by which his personality was distinguished and the effect they must have had is clear when we look at the impact of his character on history and his unique achievement in the various fields of knowledge, literature and culture.

After memorizing the Noble Qur'an, he set about memorizing *hadith* and then turned to poetry, studying language through the different periods of poetic development. Then he immersed himself in the field of Islamic culture, paying particular attention to legal judgements. He collected books and extracted all that could be extracted from them. He took a long time over the books he wrote, taking great pains in his research and accuracy so that he would produce definitive, appropriate, coherent works for people from which nothing had been left out. For that reason people were hungry for his words and his books were widely read.

Our forbears considered him, after his teacher Ibn Taymiyyah, as the Greatest Scholar, the Shaykh of Islam and the Muslims, the Seal of the Certain, the heir of the knowledge of the *mujtahids*, the leader of the intellectual renaissance in the 8th century and the saviour of the Islamic world.

---

*The meaning of italicised Arabic terms can be found in the Glossary.

FROM ONE WORLD TO ANOTHER!

'Why, but when the soul reaches the throat of the dying and at that moment you are watching - and We are nearer to him than you, but you do not see Us.'[1]

When someone dies, the Angel of Death comes to take his soul, no matter where he is. The dying person sees him, hears him, and speaks to him, but not with his eyes, his ears, or his tongue. How then? I do not know exactly. All I do know is that when he begins to move to another world, he sees, hears, and speaks, by some means which we, the living, do not perceive. Many instances of this have been recorded:

Ibn Abi'd-Dunya mentions that on the day 'Umar b. 'Abdu'l-'Aziz died, he said to those with him, 'Sit with me.' When they sat down next to him, he said, 'I am the one You commanded and I failed you. You forbade me and I rebelled.' He said this three times. Then he said, 'But there is no god but Allah.' Then he lifted his head and stared. They said, 'You are looking very intently, Amir al-Mu'minin.' He replied, 'I see a presence which is neither man nor jinn.' Then he died.

Fadala b. Dinar said, 'I was with Muhammad b. Wasi' when he was very near to death. He began to say, "Welcome to my Lord's angels! There is no strength nor power except by Allah!" I smelled the sweetest fragrance that I had ever smelled. Then his eyes glazed over and he died.'

Why do I need to look so far into the past, to the days of the first Muslims? I myself was present at the moment of

[1] Al- Waqi'a (56): 83-85

someone's death in our own time. I was with my grandmother when she was dying. It was at the time of the Dawn Prayer. She was in pain and gasping for breath, moaning from the intensity of the pain but in spite of that, she kept repeating with great joy, 'Allah! Death is sweet!' and saying the *shahada* over and over for several minutes. Then it was all over. This is where our job, those of us who are still alive, begins.

After the soul is taken, if it is a pure soul and has relatives in the Next World who are people of the Garden, they come to meet the soul with yearning and great joy. They ask it about the condition of those who are still alive in this world.

The angels then bear the soul from one heaven to the next until it comes into the presence of Allah, glory be to Him and may He be exalted! Then it returns and sees the washing of the body, its shrouding, and the funeral procession. It says either, 'Take me forward! Take me forward!' or 'Where are you taking me?' The people there cannot hear this.

When the corpse has been placed in the grave, the soul inserts itself between the body and the shroud so that the questioning can take place. Then the soul hears the receding footfall of the last of the people who followed the funeral and the earth is levelled over him. The earth, however, does not prevent the angels from reaching him. Even if a stone had been hollowed out for him and he had been placed into it and the opening sealed over with lead, it still would not stop the angels from reaching him. These dense substances cannot prevent the passage of souls. They do not even stop the *jinn*. Allah - glory be to Him! - made stone and earth the same for the angels as air is for birds.

The Grave expands and stretches for the soul, and as a result for the body as well. The body is in a grave of the narrowest dimensions and yet it expands, because of the soul, as far as the eye can see.

For details and confirmation of what I have said I will quote a sound *hadith* of the Messenger of Allah, may Allah bless him and grant him peace. He said,

> 'When the believer is about to depart from this world and go forward into the Next World, angels with faces as bright as the sun descend from the heavens and sit around him in throngs stretching as far as the eye can see. Then the Angel of Death comes and sits at his head and says, "Good soul, come out to forgiveness and pleasure from Allah!" Then his soul emerges like a drop of water flows from a water-skin and the angel takes hold of it. When he has grasped it, the other angels do not leave it in his hand even for the twinkling of an eye. They take it and place it in a perfumed shroud and a fragrance issues from it like the sweetest scent of musk found on the face on the earth.
>
> 'Then they bear it upwards and whenever they take it past a company of angels, they ask, "Who is this good soul?" and the angels with the soul reply, "So-and-so the son of so-and-so," using the best names by which people used to call him in this world. They bring him to the lowest heaven and ask for the gate to be opened for him. It is opened for him and angels who are near Allah from each of the heavens accompany him to the subsequent heaven until he reaches to the heaven where Allah the Great is. Allah, the Mighty and Majestic, says, 'Register the book of My slave in *'Illiyun* and take him back to earth. I created them from it and I return them to it and I will bring them forth from it again."
>
> 'His soul is then returned to his body and two angels come to him. They make him sit up and say to him, "Who is your Lord?" He replies, "My Lord is Allah." They ask him, "What is your religion?" He replies, "My religion is Islam." They ask him, "Who is this man who was sent among you?" He replies, "The Messenger of

Allah." They ask him, "How did you come to know these things?" He replies, "I read the Book of Allah, believed it, and declared it to be true." Then a Voice from on high declares, "My slave has spoken the truth, so spread out carpets from the Garden for him and open a gate of the Garden for him!" Then some of its fragrance and perfume comes to him, his grave is expanded for him as far as the eye can see, and a man with beautiful garments and a fragrant scent comes to him and says, "Rejoice in what delights you for this is the day which you were promised." He asks, "Who are you? Yours is a face which presages good." He replies, "I am your good actions." Then he says, "O Lord, let the Last Hour come soon so that I may rejoin my family and my property!"

'When an unbeliever is about to depart from this world and go forward into the Next World, angels with black faces descend from the heavens carrying rough hair-cloth and sit around him in throngs stretching as far as the eye can see. Then the Angel of Death comes and sits at his head and says, "Foul soul, come out to the wrath and anger of Allah!" Then his soul divides up in his body and it is dragged out like a skewer is pulled out of wet wool. Then the angel takes hold of it. When he has grasped it, the other angels do not leave it in his hand even for the twinkling of an eye. They take it and wrap it in the rough hair-cloth and a stench comes out of it like the worst stench of a corpse on the face of the earth.

'Then they take it up and whenever they take it past a company of angels, they ask, "Who is this foul soul?" and the angels with the soul reply, "So-and-so the son of so-and-so," using the worst names by which people used to call him in this world. They bring him to the lowest heaven and ask for the gate to be opened for him. It does not get opened.'

The Messenger of Allah, may Allah bless him and grant him peace, then recited, *'The gates of heaven will not be opened to them nor will they enter the Garden until the camel passes through the eye of the needle.'*[2]

'Then Allah, the Mighty and Majestic, will say, "Register his book in *Sijjin* in the lowest earth." Then his soul is flung down.'

The Prophet then recited, *'Whoever associates anything with Allah, it is as though he has fallen from heaven and the birds snatch him away or the wind sweeps him headlong into a place far away.'*[3]

'Then his soul is returned to his body and two angels come and say to him, "Who is your Lord?" He replies, "Alas, alas, I do not know!" Then a voice calls from on high, "My slave has lied, so spread out carpets from the Fire for him and open a gate of the Fire for him!" Then a hot blast from it comes to him, his grave is made so narrow for him that his ribs are pressed together, and a man with a hideous face and clothing and a foul odour comes to him and says, "Grieve on account of what has brought you disgrace for this is the day which you were promised." He asks, "Who are you? Yours is a face which presages evil." He replies, "I am your bad actions." Then he says, "O Lord, do not let the Last Hour come!"

Allah the Exalted says in His Mighty Book regarding the words used by the two angels who question the dead person in the grave, *'Allah confirms those who believe with the firm word, in the life of this world and in the Next World. Allah leads astray the wrongdoers, and Allah does whatever He will.'*[4]

---

[2] Al-A'raf (7): 40
[3] Al-Hajj (22): 31
[4] Ibrahim (14): 27

THE MEANING AND TRUTH OF DEATH

'Every soul will taste death.'[1]

What is death? Is it total annihilation? Or is it simply the severing of the soul from the body? When the soul is separated from the body, what happens to each of them? What happens to man himself, the owner of this transient body and eternal soul? Does his consciousness come to an end when his body dies? Or does his awareness continue to live on in his eternal soul? Do the dead feel enjoyment and pain the way the living do? Can the awareness of a living man whose soul is locked in his body compare with the awareness of a dead man whose soul has been released from his body?

Naturally the answer to this last question is, No! The living are aware and the dead are aware. But there is a difference and there is no way to compare them. Death is not pure annihilation. It is merely movement from one world to another. When the dead man feels the bliss or punishment of the grave, it does not mean that he is alive in his grave, needing food, clothes and so on. Nor does it mean that his soul permeates all the parts of his body as it did when he was in this world. The soul returns to the body again in a way which is not the same as in this world so that the dead man can be questioned and tested in the grave.

We can get some idea of this by likening death to sleep which is the 'lesser death', even though there is of course a natural disparity between the two. In sleep, a man's soul

---

[1] Al Imran (2): 185

comes out though his nostrils and travels until it comes into the presence of the Lord of the Throne. If the sleeper is in a state of purity, his soul prostrates before its Creator. Then it may encounter the world of dreams or meet with the souls of people who have died, but what it is in fact faced with is a page of Allah's knowledge of the Unseen containing the good or evil He has decreed for this particular human being. If the sleeper is truthful, generous, and pure, and someone who does not concern himself with stupid things during the time he is awake, then when his soul returns to him it conveys to his heart the truth of what Allah, the Great and Majestic, has let him see. When this happens, it is called a 'truthful dream'. In sleep, the soul can also move freely about the world and meet with the souls of people who are still alive and gain knowledge from them. Some of what it learns is true and some false. The false part is the normal dream or the chatter of the soul.

If the sleeper is a liar and likes what is false, his soul still rises to heaven during sleep, moves freely about the world, meets with other souls and learns true information about the Unseen. However while the soul is returning to the body, it meets *Shaytan* in mid-air and he mixes the true with the false like he does when a person is awake. Then when he wakes up, the person is confused and muddled about what Allah the Mighty and Majestic has let him see and consequently does not understand it, only remembering what *Shaytan* showed him. Those are confused dreams.

In confirmation of these things, we will mention what Allah the Great has said in the *sura, az-Zumar*, *"Allah takes the souls at the time of their death, and that which has not died, in its sleep. He withholds that against which He has decreed death, but looses the other until a stated term."*[2]

In the sleeping state, the soul does not completely leave the body as it does in the case of death, but remains inside the body not leaving it to move freely through the heavens. We can liken it to a ray or a thread whose end remains connected to the body. The ray of this soul stretches out to

[2] Az-Zumar (39): 42

the heavens and then returns again to the body when the sleeper wakes up. It is like the rays of the sun. The orb of the sun is in the heaven but its rays are on the earth. The two cases are not exactly the same, but it is a way of making the meaning clearer.

In the case of death, the body remains in the ground while the soul is in the interspace between the two worlds. An 'interspace' is something which separates two things: heaven and earth, or this world and the Next World. In other words, it is the period between death and resurrection. The bliss or punishment of the *Interspace* is not the same as the bliss and punishment of the Next World. It is something that happens between this world and the Next World. Despite the fact that the soul is in the interspace between the two worlds and the body is inside the earth, the two are still connected. Consequently, the bliss or punishment happens to both of them.

We have likened this condition to the sleeping state, but naturally there is a distinction. In sleep, the soul subsists fundamentally in the body. It emerges as something like a ray to the heavens so that the sleeper has a dream in which he feels either happy or miserable. He experiences either bliss or punishment in his sleep.

In death, the soul subsists fundamentally in the *Interspace*, not in the body. When Allah the Great desires bliss or punishment for the soul, He connects it to the body. It is in Heaven, but at the same time it looks at and is connected to the body in the ground. The soul is diffused in more than one place at the same time. The proof of this is that the Messenger, peace and blessings be upon him, saw Musa, peace and blessing be upon him, on the night of the Night Journey standing in prayer in his grave and he also saw him in the sixth and seventh heavens.

In spite of that, bliss or punishment happen at times to both body and soul simultaneously. At other times, it happens only to the soul. The dead person can lose awareness for a time but then the bliss or punishment continues. That is dependent on the will of Allah the Great and dependent on a man's own actions.

One of the people of earlier times thought that if his body were burned to ashes and then some of the ashes were cast into the sea and some onto dry land on a very windy day, he would be saved from the punishment of the grave. He therefore told his children to do that. However Allah commanded the sea to collect together the ashes that had been thrown into it and the land to do likewise and then said, 'Get up!' and the man found himself standing before Allah. Allah questioned him, asking 'What made you do what you did?' He replied, 'I feared You, my Lord, but You are the one who knows best.' Because of that Allah forgave him.

Doing that could not eliminate the punishment and the bliss of the Grave which affect those parts which no longer exist. If a righteous man were to be buried in a fiery furnace, his portion of bliss would still reach his soul and body and Allah would make the fire cool and peaceful for him. For the wrongdoer, the cool air becomes fire and hot wind. The elements and the matter of the universe obey their Lord, Originator and Creator. He makes them behave in whatever way He wills. None of them are able to do anything except what He wills. Everything obeys His will in humble submission to His decree.

THE BLISS OF THE INTERSPACE BETWEEN THE TWO WORLDS

'O soul at peace, return unto your Lord, well-pleased and well- pleasing! Enter among My slaves! Enter My Garden!'[1]

'The Grave'...the Grave is a word that inspires fear. We are pained when it is mentioned. We are not aware of the delight it can contain. Indeed, the bliss of the Grave is better than any delight that this world can offer. The Messenger, blessings and peace be upon him, said, 'When the believer is near to death, angels of mercy come to him. When his soul is taken, they place it in a piece of white silk and bear it to the gate of Heaven. They say, "We have never smelled a sweeter fragrance than this!" His soul is asked, "How is so-and-so? How is so- and-so?" It will be said, "Let him rest. He has just come from the suffering of the world!"'

The Grave or the *Interspace* is the third stage of human existence. The first is the domain of the mother's womb with all the constriction and the three darknesses it contains. The second is the domain of this world in which we grow up, which we are familiar with and from which we acquire good and evil and the means to happiness or misery. The third is the domain of the *Interspace* which is wider and vaster than the domain in which we now live - the domain of this world. The fourth and final stage is the Everlasting Domain which comprises the Garden and the Fire. There is no domain after it for it is the Domain of Eternity.

---

[1] Al-Fajr (89): 27-30.

What we are at present concerned with is the third stage, the domain of the interspace between the worlds. It is the first of the stages of the Next World. In it the souls are divided into two groups: one group is punished and imprisoned, distracted by its punishment from everything else - such as visiting or meeting each other. The other group is in bliss, and it is this second group that we are concerned with here.

The liberated souls of those who are in bliss visit each other and discuss what happened in the world they have left and the people of that world. Every soul keeps company with those of his friends who acted in a similar way to him. Many people have had dreams showing this. One such dream was recorded by Salih b. Bashir who said, 'I saw 'Ata' as-Sulami in a dream after he died and said to him, "May Allah have mercy on you! You suffered for a long time in this world!" He replied, "By Allah, that has been followed by long-lasting joy and unending delight." I asked, "What is your station?" He replied, "With those whom Allah has blessed among the prophets, the sincere, the martyrs and the righteous." '

Allah the Great says, *'Whoever obeys Allah and the Messenger, they are with those whom Allah has blessed, the prophets, the sincere, the martyrs, and the righteous. Very excellent companions they are!'*[2]

The souls who are in bliss enjoy this state from the moment of death. We have already made that clear in great detail and corroborated it with a sound *hadith*. When the believer is dying, the angels come to him and speak to him and he speaks to them without the people present being aware of this. The soul yearns to meet its Lord and leaves the body with ease. Then the angels bear it to the heavens and a sweet fragrance diffuses from it which is perceived by all the angels and the pure, liberated souls in the heavens. They ask each other about this sweet fragrance. His relatives and dearest friends who were with him in the world hasten to him. They advance before him to the next world, crowding

---

[2] An-Nisa' (4): 69

round him and asking him for news of the world and those who are in it. Then the angels take the soul up from heaven to heaven and every angel in every heaven he passes through prays for blessings on him. He is delighted by the sweetest and most beautiful good tidings. Then the soul comes to a standstill before the Almighty King, may His majesty be exalted! He says to the soul, 'Welcome to this good soul and to the body which it left.' When the Lord, the Mighty and Majestic, makes something welcome, then everything welcomes it and every constriction departs from it. Then He says, 'Show him his place in the Garden and display before him the honour and blessing I have prepared for him.' Then the angels take him back down to the earth so that he can see his body being washed and they carry on a conversation although the living cannot hear it.

The angels pray for the soul of the believer in the heavens just as people pray over his body on the earth. Finally, the body is buried and the soul returns to between the body and the shroud. This return does not imply the same connection that the soul had to the body in this world. It is not even the same connection which it had in the sleeping state nor the connection which it has when it is in its resting place. This return is a special return for the questioning as we have already clarified.

Then, as we have already mentioned, the two angels, Munkar and Nakir, come down and question him. After that a door onto the Fire is opened for him and he is told, "Look! This would have been your place in the Fire if you had rebelled against Allah and Allah had exchanged your place in the Garden for it." Then that door is locked and another door onto the Garden is opened and he sees his place there. This door will remain open until the Day of Rising. Some of the sweetness and fragrance of the Garden reaches him and his grave is made spacious. He sleeps in peace just as if he were in one of the meadows of the Garden.

This spaciousness, light and greenery in which the believer remains from the time of his death until the Day of Rising is not the same as we know in our world. If a living person were to open a grave, he would not find any expanse, light or greenness there. He would not find an open door through which he could see the Garden. He does not see bliss or torment. It is only the dead person who is aware of these things and sees them. Allah, through His wisdom, has the power to veil this from the living.

The proof that this is so is shown by the fact that there are other creatures like the *jinn* who live with us on the earth. They converse in raised voices among us but we do not see or hear them. There were angels who fought with the believers [at Badr] and struck down the unbelievers and shouted at them, but the Muslims did not see or hear them. *Jibril* came to the Messenger, blessings and peace be upon him, in the midst of the people and they did not see or hear him.

When a man is near death, the angel stretches out his hand to the soul and seizes it, speaks to it and then it comes out. A light like the sun's ray and a sweet fragrance come out to the soul. Then it ascends amid rows of angels, but those who are there cannot see or smell this. He is questioned, punished, beaten, and wails and cries out. All this happens while he is lying dead and his family are around him, but they neither hear nor see it. The sleeper dreams and enjoys his dream or is tormented by it, while someone awake at his side is not able to perceive what is going on at all.

Allah - glory be to Him and may He be exalted! - has given inanimate objects awareness and perception by which they glorify their Lord. The stones fall down out of fear of Him. The mountains and trees prostrate. The pebbles, water and plants glorify Him. All this is going on but we are not aware of it. Allah the Great said, *"There is nothing which does not glorify His praise, but you do not understand their glorification."*[3] The Companions heard the food that was being eaten glorifying Allah. That was because the Companions had a transparency of heart that does not now exist among us. All these things are part of our world and yet we are in

---

[3] Al-Isra' (17): 44

complete ignorance of them. It is not too much of an extrapolation to extend this to our being unaware of the things of the Next World.

An illustration of the bliss of the interspace between the two worlds is found in the words of the Messenger of Allah, may Allah bless him and grant him peace, regarding martyrdom. He said,

> 'The martyr receives six good things from Allah: He forgives him as soon as his blood is spilled and shows him his place in the Garden, He protects him from the punishment of the grave, He gives him security from the *Greatest Terror*, He places on his head a crown of dignity, a single ruby of which is more valuable than this world and all that it contains, He marries him to seventy-two dark-eyed houris, and He intercedes for seventy of his relatives.'

He also said,

> 'When any of your brothers is struck down (in battle), Allah puts their souls in the crops of green birds which go to the rivers of the Garden, eat its fruits and shelter in golden lamps in the shade of the Throne. When they have experienced the sweetness of their food and drink and their excellent reception, they say, "If only our brothers knew what Allah has done for us they would never abandon *jihad* nor talk about profane war instead." Allah, the Mighty and Majestic says, "I will relay this to them from you."'

Then Allah the Great revealed to His Messenger, may Allah bless him and grant him peace, *'Do not reckon those killed in the way of Allah as dead. They are alive with their Lord, provided for.'*[4]

---

[4] Al Imran (3): 169

THE PUNISHMENT OF THE INTERSPACE

'If you could only see when the wrongdoers are in the agonies of death, and the angels are stretching out their hands, 'Bring out your souls! Today you will be repaid with the punishment of humiliation.'[1]

The Grave is unknown territory. Outwardly it is quiet, but inwardly it contains secrets and terrors which an ordinary man cannot perceive. They can only be perceived by someone who has been given a high degree of belief and inner sight.

It is a strange fact that animals are able to hear the punishment in the Grave while human beings as a general rule cannot. The Prophet, may Allah bless him and grant him peace, said, 'They are punished and the animals hear it.'

Thabit al-Bunani said regarding this, 'Once I was walking among the graves and I heard a voice behind me, saying, "Thabit! Do not be deceived by their stillness. How many people in them are suffering!" I turned around, but did not see anyone.'

Al-Hasan passed a graveyard and said, 'What a host of people are here! How silent they are! How many there are among them who are suffering!'

We have already made it clear in the previous section that a dead person is either in a state of bliss or punishment, from the moment they die until the moment the two angels question them. We reached the point where a door onto the

---

[1] Al-An'am (6): 93

Garden is opened for the unbeliever and he is told to look at what his place would have been in the Garden if he had obeyed Allah. Then it is locked and another door is opened and he is told to look at his place in the Fire. It stays open and the blast of hot air from it continues to reach him until the Day of Rising. Then the earth presses in on him and he is crushed to the point that his ribs split apart. Then various forms of punishment rain down on him according to the type of wrong actions he committed.

Many statements have come down to us showing us the reality of the punishment of the Grave, or what we might also call the punishment of the interspace between the two worlds. The Prophet, may Allah bless him and grant him peace, said,

> 'I passed Badr and saw a man come out of the ground. Another man hit him with a stick until he vanished back into the earth. Then that happened again.'

The Messenger of Allah, may Allah bless him and grant him peace, went on to say,

> 'That was Abu Jahl b. Hisham who will be punished in that way until the Day of Rising.'

One of the early Muslims said, 'We passed by a certain watering-place on the way to Basra. We heard the braying of a donkey and asked the people there what the braying was. They replied that it was one of the men who used to be with them whose mother had asked him for something and he had told her to bray like a donkey. Since his death, this braying had been heard every night from his grave.'

'Amr b. Dinar said, 'The sister of one of the men of Madina died and he buried her. When he came back from the burial, he remembered that he had left something in the grave. He asked one of his companions to help him. His companion related that they had dug up the grave and found what they were looking for. Then the man said, "Let us dig further and find out what has happened to my sister." He lifted up one of the stones covering the burial cavity and found the grave filled with fire. He replaced it and filled in the grave again. Then he returned to his mother and asked, "What was my sister really like?" She replied, "Why do you ask about her when she is dead?" He said, "Tell me." She said, "She used to delay the prayer and she also used to go to our neighbours' doors, put her ear to them and then tell other people what they said!"'

There are also the *hadiths* of the Messenger, may Allah bless him and grant him peace, about the Night Journey which contain descriptions of the many types of punishment he saw in the interspace between the two worlds. We will give a summary of them here.

There are those who are driven like cattle and forced to eat herbage more bitter than aloes and the bitter fruit of *zaqqum* and driven on to the hot stones of *Jahannam* because they did not purify their property by paying *zakat*. There are those who have to eat foul putrid meat because they fornicated. There are those whose lips are cut with iron scissors because they rose to speak and address people during times of civil strife. Some of them have bellies as big as houses and whenever one of them gets up, he is knocked down and says, "O Allah, do not let the Hour come!" They are in the path of the people of Pharaoh who come and trample them while they can do nothing but scream. These are people who devoured usury.

Some of them are screaming with their mouths gaping open while they devour hot coals which come out of their anuses. These are people who consumed the property of orphans. Some of them cut pieces from their own sides and eat their own flesh. They are the slanderers and those about whom the Prophet, peace and blessings be upon him, said,

> 'We saw people cutting flesh from their sides and eating it. It was said, "As you used to consume the flesh of your brother!" I asked, "Who are they?" and I was told, "Those of your community who slandered."'

Some of them have brass nails with which they scratch their faces and chests. They are those who were backbiters and maligned people's honour.

Part of the *hadith* of the Night Journey is...

> 'Some people were cracking open their heads with a stone. Every time they did this, their heads were restored to what they were like in the first place. This went on and on without stopping. I said, "Jibril, who are they?" Jibril replied, "They are people who turned away from the prayer."'

One of the Prophet's dreams - and the dreams of the Prophets are true and a part of revelation which gets right to the heart of the matter - was related as follows. He said,

> 'Last night, I saw two men who came to me and took me by the hand and brought me to the Holy Land. I could see one man sitting and another man standing holding an iron hook which he stuck into the side of the sitting man's mouth so that it came out at the back of his neck. Then he did the same to the other side. After his mouth had healed itself and gone back to normal, he did the same thing all over again. I asked what this was and they told me to go on.

> 'We went on until we came to a man lying on his back. Another man was standing at his head with a stone or a rock with which he smashed it. When he hit the head, the stone rolled away and he went to recover it. He did not get back to the man until his head had mended and returned to normal, then he smashed it again. I asked what this was and they told me to go on.

> 'We came to a hole like a furnace which was narrow at the top and wide at the bottom. There was a fire burning under it and there were naked men and women in it. The flames leapt up to them from underneath. When the fire came near, they rose up

until they almost came out. When it abated, they went back into it again. I asked what this was and they told me to go on.

We went on until we came to a river of blood with a man standing in it. On the bank of the river there was a man with some stones in front of him. The man in the river came forward and when he was about to get out, the man threw a stone at him and he went back to where he had been before. Every time he went to come out, the man threw a stone at him and he went back to where he had been before. I asked what this was and they told me to go on.

'We went on until we came to a green garden with an enormous tree in it, under which there was an old man and some children. Near the tree there was a man kindling a fire in front of him. They took me up the tree and into a house more beautiful than any I had ever seen. There were old men and youths in it. Then they took me up and brought me into another house which was even more beautiful. I said to my companions, "You have been with me for the whole night, so now tell me about what I have seen."

'They replied, "Certainly! The man you saw whose mouth was being pierced was the originator of a lie, which spread from him to all parts of the earth. He will suffer like that until the Day of Rising. The one whose head was being smashed was a man who had learned the Qur'an but had spent his nights asleep and did not act according to it during the daytime. He will suffer like that until the Day of Rising. The people in the hole were fornicators. The man you saw in the river devoured usury. The old man at the foot of the tree was Ibrahim and the children around him were mankind's children. The one kindling the fire was Malik, the Guardian of the Fire. The first house was that of the ordinary believers and this house is the house of the martyrs. I am *Jibril* and this is *Mika-'il*."

'He lifted his head and I did likewise. I saw a castle like a cloud and they told me that it was my dwelling. I asked them to let me enter my dwelling. They replied that my life was not yet completed, but that when my life had come to an end, I would enter my dwelling."'

The Prophet, may Allah bless him and grant him peace, said regarding seeking refuge from the punishment of the Interspace or the Grave,

'When any of you finishes the final *tashahhud*, he should seek refuge with Allah from four things: from the punishment of *Jahannam*, the punishment of the Grave, the trials of the living and the dead, and the trials of the *Dajjal*.'

All of this shows that the punishment of the Grave is true beyond any doubt. We will add what Allah says about the two punishments - the punishment of the *Interspace* and the punishment of the Day of Rising:

'*...the Fire, to which they will be exposed morning and evening, and on the day when the Hour comes, 'Admit the people of Pharaoh to the most severe punishment!'*[2] and also '*Whoever turns away from My remembrance will have a life of narrowness and We shall gather him blind on the Day of Rising.*'[3]

---

[2] Ghafir (40): 46

[3] Taha (20): 124

HOW CAN A MAN SAVE HIMSELF FROM THE PUNISHMENT OF THE INTERSPACE BEFORE IT IS TOO LATE?

'Race to forgiveness from your Lord, and a Garden whose breadth is like the breadth of the heaven and the earth.'[1]

Outwardly the Grave is stillness while inwardly it is either punishment or bliss. The intelligent man is the one who protects himself against the evil of this punishment before it is too late. Such a man knows with certainty that sooner or later his day will come, and that this moment is known only to the Almighty Creator. It might come without warning. When it comes a man leaves behind all the wealth he has amassed and moves to another world. Only there will he feel regret, but regret then will not do him any good. In that place, only good actions are of any use. They alone will be useful currency on that critical day. Only with them will he be able to purchase a magnificent mansion in the Garden with all the luxuries and blessings it contains, an everlasting mansion, not one which disappears as things do in this world.

The intelligent man is the one who acts for this world as if he were going to live forever and acts for the Next World as if he were going to die tomorrow. To confirm what I have said, I will recall a dream of the Messenger, remembering that all the dreams of the prophets are true. He had a dream in which he saw one of the muslims. The Angel of Death came

---

[1] Al-Hadid (57): 21

to take his soul but his correct behaviour towards his parents came and drove the Angel of Death away from him. He saw another of the Muslims surrounded by shaytans. Then his remembrance of Allah came and made the shaytans fly from him. Then he saw a third muslim surrounded by the angels of punishment. His prayer came and rescued him from their hands. The tongue of a fourth muslim was lolling out from thirst and whenever he approached a pool of water, he was stopped and driven away. Then his fasting of Ramadan came and gave him water to drink. He saw another man and the prophets sitting in circles. Everytime the muslim approached one of the circles, he was stopped and driven away. His ghusl for janaba came, took hold of his hand, and sat him down in the circle. Another muslim had darkness in front of him, behind him, on his right, on his left and above him. He was completely lost in it. Then his hajj and 'umra came and led him out of the darkness into the light. Another muslim was being pursued by flames and sparks of fire. His sadaqa formed a veil between him and the fire and shaded his head. Another muslim was speaking to a group of believers who would not speak to him. His upholding of kinship came and told the group of believers that he had maintained ties of kinship and ordered them to speak to him. Then the believers spoke to him and shook hands with him. Another muslim was surrounded by the *Zabaniyya* (angels of *Jahannam*). His commanding the right and forbidding the wrong came and rescued him from them and put him among the angels of mercy. Another muslim was kneeling with a veil between him and Allah. His good character came, took his hand and Allah let him enter His presence. Another muslim had received his book in his left hand. His fear of Allah came and took his book and placed it in his right hand. The scales of another muslim were light in the balance. Those of his children who had died young came and made the scales level. Another muslim was standing on the brink of *Jahannam*. His hope in Allah came and rescued him from it, and he withdrew from it. Another muslim had fallen into the Fire. The tears that he had wept out of fear of

Allah came and rescued him from it. Another muslim was standing on the *Sirat* trembling like a leaf in a strong wind. His good opinion of Allah came and his terror was allayed and he was able to go on. Another muslim was crawling on the Sirat, sometimes creeping and sometimes just clinging on. His prayer came and put him on his feet and rescued him. Another muslim reached the gates of the Garden but they were locked against him. His testimony that there is no god but Allah came and opened the gates for him and let him into the Garden.

> The Prophet also said regarding the *sura*, *al-Mulk*,
> 'This sura has thirty ayats which intercede for anyone who knows them until they receive forgiveness, *"Blessed be He in whose hand is the Kingdom."* [2]

Among the dreams of the early muslims is one related by Yazid b. Nu'ama who said, 'A girl died in the al-Jarif plague. Her father met her in a dream after her death and asked her to tell him about the Next World. She replied, "My father, this is a big subject you have raised. We know but cannot act. You can act but do not know. By Allah, one or two acts of glorification and one or two rak'ats of the prayer in the book of my actions are preferable to me than the world and all it contains."'

The Grave has an embrace from which neither believer or unbeliever can escape. Afterwards, the believer is relieved of its pressure while the unbeliever remains in punishment. The Messenger of Allah, may Allah bless him and grant him peace, said,

> 'The Grave has a pressure and if anyone were to be saved from it, it would be Sa'd b. Mu'adh.'

The wisdom of the pressure and embrace of the Grave is in what Ibn Abi'd-Dunya related from Muhammad at-Taymi. He said that the people say that the earth is their mother. They were created from it and they were away from it for a long time. Then when they return to it, it embraces them as a

---

[2] Al-Mulk (67): 1

mother embraces her child when it has been away for a long time and then returns to her. Whoever obeyed Allah is embraced with compassion and tenderness. Whoever disobeyed Allah is embraced with harshness because the earth is angry with him for the sake of its Lord.

When 'Abdu'l-'Aziz b. Sulayman al-'Abid died, one of his companions saw him in a dream wearing a green garment with a crown of pearls on his head. He asked him how he was and what the experience of the taste of death was like and what things were like where he was. He replied, 'Do not ask about the intensity of the grief and sorrow of death! However, Allah's mercy concealed all our faults and we encountered nothing but His bounty.'

The Prophet, peace and blessings be upon him, said,

> 'Allah has forbidden the earth to consume the bodies of the prophets.'

He also said,

> 'No-one prays for peace on me without Allah addressing my soul so that I return the greeting to him.'

He also said,

> 'Whenever any man visits the grave of his brother and sits with him, he is keeping company with him until he gets up to go.'

He taught his community to say when they visit people's graves,

> 'Peace be upon you, people who dwell here, both believers and Muslims. If Allah wills, we will join you. May Allah have mercy on those who have gone ahead and those who have stayed behind. We ask Allah for well-being for both you and us.'

WHAT CAN THE LIVING DO TO RESCUE THE DEAD PERSON FROM PUNISHMENT?

'To Allah belongs the intercession altogether. To Him belongs the kingdom of the heavens and the earth.'[1]

We will refer back to the first sentence in the first section: 'The living go on and the dead do not.'

A man is living in our midst. Suddenly death snatches him from us. We wail and wear black. We set up the funeral tents and so forth. In short, we do what is necessary. Then we forget him on the premise that 'The living go on and the dead do not.' Or else we continue to remember him and abandon ourselves to our grief, living a life of constant anguish, claiming to be faithful to the dead. So our life is spent either in forgetfulness or grief. However, life is short. There is no time in it for either forgetfulness or grief. Real life does not consist of forgetfulness. Real fidelity is not to persist in grief.

Let us consider together how we can help the dead person who has left us. How can we support him in that severe trial? He is in fact in greater need of us than the living. He is now alone, buried in a grave inside the earth. The possibility of action is now finished for him. His subterfuges have come to an end. However, the benefit he can derive from actions which the living perform on his behalf have not come to an end, provided that Allah gives permission, since Allah said in His Mighty Book, *'Who will intercede with Him except by His permission?'*[2]

[1] Az-Zumar (39): 44

[2] Al-Baqara (2): 255

The Messenger of Allah, may Allah bless him and grant him peace, said,

> 'When a man dies, his actions cease except for three things: a sadaqa which goes on, knowledge which continues to benefit people or a righteous son who makes supplication for him.'

There are many things which the living can do to rescue the dead. They include supplication for them, asking forgiveness for them, acts of generosity, *hajj*, fasting and other sorts of worship. These can be attributed to the dead person with Allah's permission.

Even more important than all these is to settle the dead person's debts, whether that debt be financial or spiritual - debts to other living persons or debts of worship owed to Allah the Great.

When someone who is alive intercedes for a dead person who is being punished, his punishment is halted, even if only for a time. When he intercedes for the person enjoying bliss, that person is raised a degree.

Ibn Abi'd-Dunya mentioned that one of his companions said, 'My brother died and I saw him in a dream. I said, "How was it when you were placed in your grave?" He replied, "Someone brought me a fiery flame and if it had not been that someone else made supplication for me, I think he would have hit me with it." '

Bashar b. Ghalib said, 'I saw Rabi'a, on whose behalf I used to make frequent supplication, in a dream. She said to me, "Bashar b. Ghalib! Your gifts have been brought to me on plates of light, covered in silken cloths." I asked, "How can that be?" She replied, "That is what the supplication of living believers is like. When they make supplication for a dead person, that supplication is answered for them on plates of light, veiled in silken cloths. Then they are brought to the dead person for whom the supplication was said and they are told, 'This is the gift of so-and-so to you.'" '

'Amr b. Jarir said that when one of Allah's servants supplicates for his dead brother, an angel takes this supplication to him in his grave and says, "You stranger in the grave! Here is a gift from a brother who feels compassion for you!"'

The Messenger of Allah, may Allah bless him and grant him peace, said,

> 'After he has died, the believer only gets the benefit of the following actions and good deeds: knowledge which he has taught and passed on, a righteous son he leaves behind, a copy of the Qur'an which he has bequeathed, a mosque he has built, a house he has built for the traveller, a water channel he has dug, or an act of charity which he spent out of his property when he was alive and in good health and which comes to him after his death.'

The Qur'an says, *'Those who have come after them say, "Our Lord, forgive us and our brothers who preceded us in belief."*[3] Allah - glory be to Him! - praised them for asking for forgiveness for the believers before them. He indicated that they are helped when the living ask for forgiveness for them.

The Prophet, may Allah bless him and grant him peace, said,

> 'When you pray over a dead person, make sincere supplication for him.'

In his supplication he would say,

> 'O Allah! So-and-so the son of so-and-so is in Your custody and near to You. Protect him from the trial of the Grave and the punishment of the Fire. You are worthy of fidelity and truth, so forgive him and show mercy to him. You are Forgiving, Merciful.'

When the Prophet, blessings and peace be upon him,

---

[3] Al-Hashr (59): 10

finished burying someone who had died, he stood over him and said,

> 'Ask forgiveness for your brother. Ask for him to be made firm. He is being questioned now.'

He also said,

> 'Teach your dead the words, "There is no god but Allah."'

There is a report from Abu Hurayra, may Allah be pleased with him, about the reward of acts of charity reaching the dead.

> Abu Hurayra said that a man said to the Prophet, may Allah bless him and grant him peace, 'My father has died and left some property, but he did not leave a will. Will he be rewarded if I make an act of charity on his behalf?' He replied, 'Yes.'

The Prophet, peace and blessings be upon him, said about the reward of fasting reaching the dead person,

> 'If someone dies and owes some days of fasting, then his heir should fast on his behalf.'

He also said,

> 'If someone dies and owes a month's fast, his heir should feed a poor person for him for every day he owes.'

As regards the reward of the *hajj* reaching a dead person,

> Ibn 'Abbas, may Allah be pleased with him, said, 'A man asked, "Prophet of Allah! My father has died and has not done the *hajj*. Shall I do it on his behalf?" He replied, "Do you not think that if your father had a debt, you would pay it for him?" He replied, "Yes." The Prophet said, "A debt that is owed to Allah is even more worthy of being paid."'

The Muslims are agreed about paying debts for which a dead person is still responsible, even if the person who pays it is a stranger and the money does not come out of the inheritance. This is indicated in the *hadith* of Abu Qatada.

> Abu Qatada said he would pay two dinars on behalf of a particular dead person. When he had paid them, the Prophet, may Allah bless him and grant him peace, said to him, 'Now his skin is cool.'

They are agreed that when someone who is alive has a claim against a dead person, any muslim is allowed to help him and discharge the debt as they would if the debt was owed by a living person.

The Messenger, blessings and peace be upon him, said,

> 'Recite the *sura*, *Yasin* when your people die.'

This can be taken to mean that it should be recited to the person when he is near death and it can also be taken to mean that it should be recited at his grave. The first possibility is more likely because the dying person benefits from the *tawhid*, the good news that the people of tawhid go to the Garden and the delight of the person who dies in upholding the knowledge of tawhid that this sura contains. It says, '*Ah, would that my people knew that my Lord has forgiven me and that He has placed me among the honoured.*'[4] The soul rejoices at this and desires to meet Allah as Allah desires to meet it. This sura is the heart of the Qur'an and something wonderful occurs when it is recited in the presence of a dying person.

Speaking in general terms, recitation of the Qur'an is one of the acts of worship whose reward reaches the dead person, provided that the reciter first intercedes with Allah on his behalf. Allah might or might not accept it, as is the case with all other acts of worship. He might accept one man's *hajj*, but not that of another man. He might accept the prayer of one man and not that of another man. What

---

[4] Yasin (36): 26-27

counts is the sincere intention to do the action for the sake of Allah the Great alone.

Let us imagine a group of Muslims who have gathered together to remember someone who was dear to them and has died. They are still wearing black and their grief is still fresh. They have gathered for the sake of the love and comradeship that exists between them to remember Allah and to intercede with Him on behalf of their loved one.

This gathering might take place anywhere, but let it be the home of one of them. Each of them is holding a copy of the Qur'an whose recitation they have divided up between themselves. They begin the recitation with the intention of directing its reward to the dead person. This does not diminish the reward that any of them receive in any way, but the reward also reaches the dead person in his grave if Allah so wills. There is a reward for both the living and the dead.

Included among those people might be a son or grandson of the dead person. This is an extension of his actions and a result of his efforts in this world, for he left a righteous son there and consequently righteous descendants. There might be a brother, a father, a relative or a friend among them which is an indication of his good behaviour with other people, otherwise they would not mention him in their supplication, or remember him or intercede on his behalf with the Lord of Might and Majesty. This is also the result of the dead man's own actions.

A righteous son or daughter is a true treasure for a man and profits him during his lifetime and after his death. Every father or mother should try as hard as they possibly can to bring up righteous children. Every son should try to obey his parents during their lifetime and after their death. It must be realised that a dead person knows what his living relatives and brothers are doing. It is said that a man in his grave delights in the righteousness of his children after him.

We could go on and on. Discussion about the soul, the dead and the Next World is unending. It is a subject which has been thoroughly studied for hundreds of years. In spite of that, we still have not plumbed its depths. We have only skimmed the surface of real knowledge of it. Only Allah - glory be to Him and may He be exalted! - has complete knowledge of it.

Whoever says, 'I know', is ignorant. I have discovered from my own experience that whenever someone increases in knowledge, they discover how much greater their ignorance is.

The words of Allah are true when He says, *'They will ask you about the spirit. Say, 'The spirit is at the behest of your Lord. You have been given but little knowledge.'* [5]

---

[5] Al-Isra' (17): 85

GLOSSARY

Ayat	A verse of the Noble Qur'an.
Dajjal	The false Messiah whose appearance marks the imminent end of the world.
Deen	The religion of Islam, stressing its all-inclusive nature.
Hadith	A report of what the Messenger of Allah, Muhammad, peace and blessings be upon him, said, did, or allowed to be done.
Hajj	The annual pilgrimage to Makka and the rites connected with it.
'Illiyun	One of the highest levels of paradise.
Jahannam	A general name for Hellfire.
Jibril	The Archangel Gabriel.
Jihad	Struggle, particularly warfare to defend and establish Islam.
Jinn	Unseen beings who co-habit the earth together with mankind.
Kunya	Cognomen used with both affection and respect.
Mika'il	The Archangel Michael.
Mujtahid	Scholar who is qualified to the extent of being able to make new precedents in the implementation of Islamic law.

Sadaqa	Voluntary charity given to gain Divine pleasure.
Shahada	The testimony that there is no god but Allah and that Muhammad is the Messenger of Allah.
Shaytan	Satan, the Devil.
Sijjin	One of the depths of Hellfire.
Sirat	A path, particularly the narrow bridge that passes over Hellfire, which all those destined to enter Paradise must cross.
Sunna	The practice of the Messenger of Allah and what he approved for his Companions.
Sura	A chapter of the Qur'an.
Tashahhud	What is said in the sitting position in the final part of the prayer.
Tawhid	The doctrine of the Divine Unity.
'Umra	A visit to Makka combined with certain prescribed rites.
Zakat	Wealth tax payable yearly as a religious duty.
Zaqqum	A tree in Hellfire, bearing fruit of extreme bitterness.